IRELAND

By Sherra G. Edgar

Published by The Child's World®
1980 Lookout Drive • Mankato, MN 56003-1705
800-599-READ • www.childsworld.com

Acknowledgments
The Child's World®: Mary Berendes, Publishing Director
Red Line Editorial: Editorial direction
The Design Lab: Design
Amnet: Production

Design elements: Shutterstock Images; Brendan Howard/
Shutterstock Images
Photographs ©: Shutterstock Images, cover (left top), cover
(left center), cover (right), 1 (top), 1 (bottom left), 10, 15
(left), 15 (right), 23, 24, 30; Brendan Howard/Shutterstock
Images, cover (left bottom), 1 (bottom right); Derek Redican/
iStockphoto, 5; Photodisc/Thinkstock, 6–7; Stefano Viola/
Shutterstock Images, 8; Joel James/iStockphoto, 11; Gary
Andrews/Shutterstock Images, 12; STR/EPA/epa/Corbis,
13; David Soanes/Shutterstock Images, 16–17; Martina I.
Meyer/Shutterstock Images, 18; iStockphoto, 20; Worytko
Pawel/Shutterstock Images, 21; Dermot McBrierty/
Shutterstock Images, 25; Patricia Hofmeester/Shutterstock
Images, 26; Wavebreak Media/Thinkstock, 27; Jaroslava
V./Shutterstock Images, 28

ISBN 9781634070485
LCCN 2014959738

Printed in the United States of America
PA02346

ABOUT THE AUTHOR

Sherra G. Edgar lives in Lumberton, Texas. She has taught primary school for 19 years and has written books for children for three years. Edgar enjoys spending time with family and friends, reading, and watching movies.

EIRE 44

ONE WORLD • COUNTRIES

TABLE OF CONTENTS

CHAPTER 1

WELCOME TO IRELAND! 5

CHAPTER 2

THE LAND 8

CHAPTER 3

GOVERNMENT AND CITIES 13

CHAPTER 4

PEOPLE AND CULTURES 20

CHAPTER 5

DAILY LIFE 25

FAST FACTS, 30

GLOSSARY, 31

TO LEARN MORE, 32

INDEX, 32

ARCTIC
OCEAN

ATLANTIC
OCEAN

PACIFIC
OCEAN

PACIFIC
OCEAN

INDIAN
OCEAN

IRELAND

SCALE

0   1000 Miles

0   1000 KM

N
W   E
S

SOUTHERN
OCEAN

IRELAND

ÉIRE   44

FUN FACT

ONE WORLD · COUNTRIES

Ireland covers about
80 percent of the
island it occupies.
The remaining part
of the island belongs
to Northern Ireland,
which is a separate
country.

CHAPTER 1

WELCOME TO IRELAND!

The air is crisp and cool in Limerick, Ireland. Families line the streets, enjoying many activities. There is colorful art everywhere. Music fills the air. Performers encourage children to dance.

Greetings from Ireland!

The music and dance are part of the Limerick Children's Festival. It takes place every October. During the whole month, children experience art, music, dance, and theater in Limerick and across the rest of Ireland.

Ireland is known for its beauty. Mountains covered with green trees and grasses roll across the country. In the cities, old castles and churches dot the land. Roads wind through wide-open spaces. The River Shannon flows across Ireland and empties into the Atlantic Ocean.

This beautiful green land is home to many people. They have created a culture

based on religion, family, and ancient traditions. Many of these traditions are still alive in Ireland today.

The heavy fog, bright green grasses, and steep cliffs of Killarney are typical of Ireland's land.

CHAPTER 2

THE LAND

The plains in central Ireland are used as pastures for the many cows and sheep raised in the country.

Ireland is an island in the Atlantic Ocean. It is off the northwest coast of Europe. Ireland's closest neighbor is Northern Ireland. Both countries share the island. England, Wales, and Scotland are nearby, too. They are east of Ireland.

Central Ireland, is low and flat. This area has lakes, **bogs**, and grasslands. Mountains form a ring around the flat land. Macgillycuddy's Reeks mountain range has the country's highest peak. It is called Carrantuohill. It is 3,406 feet high (1,038 m).

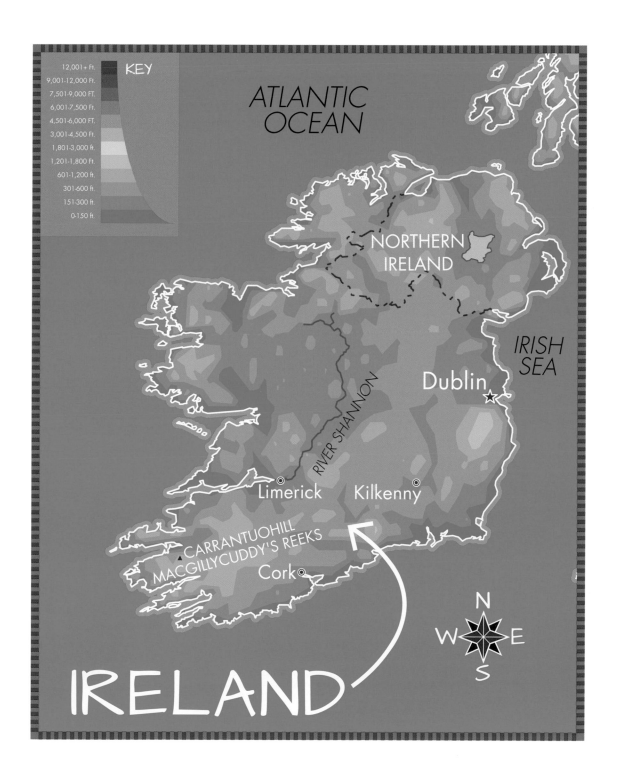

KEY

12,001+ Ft.
9,001-12,000 Ft.
7,501-9,000 Ft.
6,001-7,500 Ft.
4,501-6,000 Ft.
3,001-4,500 Ft.
1,801-3,000 ft.
1,201-1,800 ft.
601-1,200 ft.
301-600 ft.
151-300 ft.
0-150 ft.

ATLANTIC OCEAN

NORTHERN IRELAND

IRISH SEA

RIVER SHANNON

Dublin

Limerick

Kilkenny

CARRANTUOHILL
MACGILLYCUDDY'S REEKS
Cork

IRELAND

N W E S

Streams and rivers run down the mountains. The longest of these is the River Shannon. It flows for 224 miles (360 km) before draining into the Atlantic Ocean. The River Shannon is known for its salmon. Each spring, they swim from the ocean back to the river to lay their eggs.

The weather in Ireland is often rainy. Most of the country gets between 30 and 50 inches (76 and 127 cm) of rain each year. Fog is also common, most often on fall and winter mornings. The fog is heaviest in low areas.

Thick fog makes it hard to see the Galway Cathedral.

Temperatures in Ireland are mild. It is neither very cold nor very hot. The average temperature is 50 degrees Fahrenheit (10 °C).

Ireland is full of natural resources. Ireland has long been a mining country. Ireland ranks tenth in the world for the production of zinc. This is a type of metal found along the western coast of Ireland. Zinc is used in some kinds of

FUN FACT • ONE WORLD • MANY COUNTRIES

ÉIRE 44

Ireland's nickname is the Emerald Isle. That is because grasslands cover the country. They are bright green, just like an emerald.

batteries and light bulbs. A form of zinc, zinc oxide, is found in many paints.

Central Ireland is rich in peat. Peat comes from swamps and bogs. It is a type of fuel made from **decomposed** plants. When peat is dried, people burn it to heat their homes.

To harvest peat, farmers cut into the bog with a hoe. The peat is then cut into bricks, stacked, and dried.

CHAPTER 3

GOVERNMENT AND CITIES

Ireland has been an independent country since 1921. That year, it gained its freedom from the United Kingdom. Today, Ireland is divided into 28 counties. Each county has a local government.

Irish citizens in Cork go to the polls to elect government leaders in 2011.

Ireland's national government is a republic. The Irish people elect leaders to represent them in the government. They elect lawmakers and the nation's president.

The president works with lawmakers, selects judges, and appoints the prime minister. Lawmakers give the president advice on whom to choose. The prime minister is the most powerful leader in Ireland. He or she is called the *taoiseach*, which means "chief" in Irish.

Ireland's government meets in Dublin. It is the nation's capital. Dublin is also the largest city in Ireland. About 1.1 million people live there.

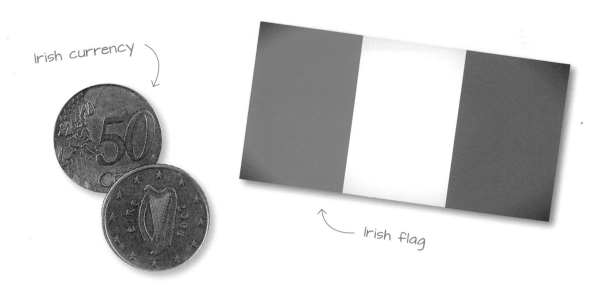

Irish currency

Irish flag

Dublin is on the east coast of Ireland, along the Irish Sea. It is the country's main port. This is where goods go in and out of Ireland. Another major waterway in Dublin is the River Liffey. It divides the city into two parts. Many bridges connect the north side with the south side.

Dublin has many historic buildings. It has two **medieval** churches, Christ's Church Cathedral and St. Patrick's Cathedral. They have stood in Dublin for nearly 1,000 years. These churches are still used today. Dublin Castle is another historic building in the city. It has been built and rebuilt since the early 1200s.

Like Dublin, the city of Cork has many landmarks. The most famous of these is the Blarney Stone at Blarney Castle. The Blarney Stone is a big piece of limestone. It is built into the wall around the castle. A legend says that kissing the stone will give a person the gift of gab. Someone with this gift is a powerful speaker.

Ireland's economy is growing fast. Farming is important for Ireland. Farmers grow potatoes, sugar beets, wheat, and barley. Many Irish farmers also raise cows. About 80 percent of the meat and milk from the cows is **exported**.

Dublin's River Liffey divides the city into north and south sides.

Ireland exports other products, too. Computers and software made in Ireland are shipped all over the world. Ireland also exports food, drinks, chemicals, plastics, and minerals. Ireland's biggest trading partners are the United States and the United Kingdom.

Ireland has more cows than people. In some parts of Ireland, such as Kerry, there are three cows for every person!

FUN FACT · ONE WORLD · COUNTRIES

ÉIRE 44

GLOBAL CONNECTIONS

During the 1840s, Ireland had a **famine**. The country's potato crops failed for three years in a row. Potatoes were the main food for Irish people at that time. Many Irish people did not have enough to eat.

As a result, more than half of the people in Ireland left their country. About 2 million Irish people **immigrated** to the United States. They hoped to find better conditions there. Instead, they found **discrimination**.

Americans treated the Irish poorly for many reasons. The Irish were Catholic, and most Americans were not. Americans did not trust the Irish because of their religion. Some people thought the Irish immigrants were taking jobs away from Americans. To stop this, businesses hung signs that said "NINA." That stood for "No Irish Need Apply".

Gradually Irish immigrants were accepted in American society. Their children and grandchildren grew up to be important writers, artists, and politicians. One of the best-known Irish American leaders was John F. Kennedy. He was the 35th president of the United States.

Today about 40 million Americans have Irish roots. That number is larger than the total number of people living in Ireland today.

CHAPTER 4

PEOPLE AND CULTURES

In Ireland, road signs are written in both English and Irish. Irish is also called Gaelic.

Ireland is a blend of different groups that have lived there. One of the earliest groups was the Celts. They were later joined by Norsemen from Norway, the French from Normandy, and the English and Scottish from Great Britain.

Over time, these groups have created modern Ireland. It has two official languages. They are English and Irish. Irish was the first national language of Ireland. It was widely spoken until the 1840s. English slowly took over, and today few people speak Irish.

Religion is also important in Ireland. Four out of five Irish people are Catholic. The Catholic Church plays an important role in the country. It oversees many of the country's schools, hospitals, and charities.

The Catholic Church is also involved in the country's national holiday, St. Patrick's Day. It is held every year on March 17. This

These Irish girls are celebrating their first communion. It is a special ceremony in the Catholic Church, which is usually held when children are seven years old.

holiday honors St. Patrick, the patron saint of Ireland. In the 400s, St. Patrick came to Ireland and told people about Christianity. People honor him with church services, prayers, and feasts.

Christmas is another important holiday in Ireland. People decorate by hanging wreaths of holly on their front doors. They also set up Christmas trees and put candles on windowsills. Many families attend church services at midnight on Christmas Eve. In the morning, children open gifts.

Besides celebrating holidays, the Irish also enjoy music. Irish music is played on the harp, bagpipes, fiddle, and accordion. The lively music is good for dancing. Irish dancers keep their upper bodies straight while doing fast footwork.

Irish dancing gained popularity outside of Ireland in the 1990s. During that time, a group called Riverdance toured the world. They showed people what Irish dancing looked like. The performances were popular. They led to the founding of many Irish dance studios throughout the world.

Dancing is not the only part of Irish culture that is well known. Many people also know about Irish **folklore**, especially leprechauns. A leprechaun is a fairy who takes the form of an old man who is a shoemaker.

Irish dancers can wear soft shoes or hard shoes. This dancer is wearing hard shoes, which create clicking and tapping sounds when the dancer moves.

According to folklore, a leprechaun has a secret pot of gold. If a leprechaun is caught, he will tell where his gold is hidden. But the leprechaun is tricky. He makes the person who caught him look away. Then he disappears without sharing his gold.

FUN FACT

According to legend, St. Patrick drove all the snakes out of Ireland. The legend says he put all the snakes in a box and threw it into the Irish Sea. Some people believe this is why Ireland has no snakes, and why the Irish Sea is so rough.

CHAPTER 5

DAILY LIFE

A traditional Irish cottage has a thatched roof.

Irish people live in a variety of houses. In the country, a traditional home is a small cottage. In the past, cottages were often made of clay or stone. Straw covered the roofs. Homes often had split doors. The bottom could stay closed, while the top could open. This allowed fresh air in, but kept animals out.

In the cities, homes are often connected in long rows. Some are painted in bright, cheery colors. Even homes that are not painted brightly often have brightly colored doors. Some people think this is to brighten the homes during the gray, rainy weather.

Large cities such as Dublin have buses, taxies, cars, and trains. Ireland also has a large network of roads. People usually drive cars or take trains when they go from city to city.

Colorful row houses line a street in Dublin.

Aran sweaters are special to Ireland. They were first made on the Aran Islands, just off the west coast of Ireland. The people who lived there were fishermen and farmers. They spent many days working outdoors in the cold, wind, and rain. They created the sweaters to protect themselves from the weather.

Aran sweaters are made of wool. The designs on Aran sweaters are often very detailed.

Along with the Aran sweater, Ireland is often associated with potatoes. Many dishes in Ireland use potatoes. Champ is a dish made of mashed potatoes and green onions. Colcannon is mashed potatoes mixed with either cabbage or kale. Stews made from lamb, potatoes, onions, and carrots are also common.

Ireland's seas provide food such as cod, salmon, and oysters. The country's many farms provide meat. Beef, pork, and lamb are all common in Irish meals.

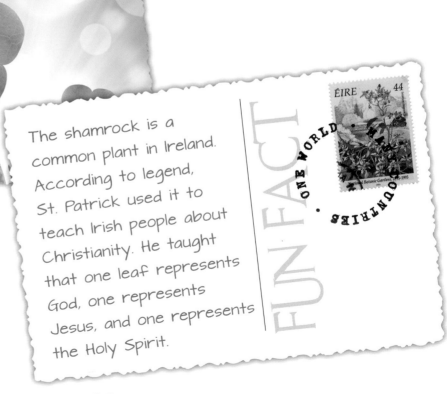

FUN FACT

The shamrock is a common plant in Ireland. According to legend, St. Patrick used it to teach Irish people about Christianity. He taught that one leaf represents God, one represents Jesus, and one represents the Holy Spirit.

Meals away from home are often eaten in a pub. Ireland has about 10,000 pubs. They are an important part of Irish social life. Pubs are where people meet friends, eat a meal, and listen to music. While there, people often take part in *craic*. It is an Irish word that describes joking and telling stories.

Ireland is a country with strong religious beliefs, ancient castles, and green hills. Its people look forward to a bright future.

DAILY LIFE FOR CHILDREN

All Irish children must start school by age six. The schools they attend are often run by churches. This means the school day often includes prayer. The students study Irish, reading, math, spelling, history, and social science.

After school, some children play sports such as Gaelic football. It is a mix of soccer and rugby. There are 15 players on each team. They score by putting the ball between two goal posts. They cannot throw the ball. It has to be kicked, punched, or punted.

FAST FACTS

Population: 4 million

Area: 32,595 square miles (84,420 sq km)

Capital: Dublin

Largest Cities: Dublin, Cork, and Limerick

Form of Government: Republic

Languages: English and Irish

Trading Partners: The United States, the United Kingdom, and Germany

Major Holidays:
St. Patrick's Day and Christmas

National Dish: Irish Stew (lamb or beef, potatoes, onions, and carrots)

Irish children often wear uniforms to school.

GLOSSARY

bogs (BOGZ) Bogs are wet, spongy areas of land made of dead plants. Bogs are common in Ireland.

decomposed (dee-kuhm-POZD) Something that has decomposed has broken down or become rotten. Peat is made up of decomposed plants.

discrimination (diss-krim-uh-NAY-shun) Discrimination is the act of treating people unfairly based on differences in race, culture, or age. Irish immigrants in the United States faced discrimination.

exported (ek-SPORT-id) Goods that have been sold to another country have been exported. Ireland has exported many goods.

famine (FAM-uhn) A famine is a shortage of food. Ireland had a famine in the 1840s.

folklore (FOHK-lohr) Folklore are stories, customs, and beliefs that are handed down from adults to children. Irish folklore includes leprechauns.

immigrated (IM-uh-grayt-id) To have immigrated is to have moved to another country to live. Many Irish people immigrated to the United States in the 1840s.

medieval (mee-DEE-vuhl) Something that is medieval comes from the Middle Ages, from 500 to 1500 AD. Ireland has medieval churches.

To Learn More

BOOKS

Levy, Patricia. *Ireland*. New York:
Cavendish Square Publishing, 2015.

Malachy, Doyle. *Tales from Old Ireland*.
Cambridge, MA: Barefoot Books, 2008.

Wallenfeldt, Jeffrey H. *Ireland*. New York:
Britannica Educational Publishing, 2014.

WEB SITES

Visit our Web site for links about Ireland: childsworld.com/links

Note to Parents, Teachers, and Librarians: We routinely verify our Web links to make sure they are safe and active sites. So encourage your readers to check them out!

Index

climate, 10–11
Cork, 17

dance, 5–6, 22
Dublin, 15–17, 26

economy, 17–18

folklore, 22, 24
food, 28

holidays, 21–22
homes, 25–26

immigration, 19

languages, 21
Limerick, 5–6

music, 5–6, 22

religion, 7, 21, 29
River Liffey, 16
River Shannon, 6, 10

schools, 29